AF083610

SHORT WALKS IN DUMFRIES & GALLOWAY

by Ronald Turnbull

Penkiln Burn, Newton Stewart (Walk 4)

CONTENTS

Using this guide	4
Route summary table	6
Map key	7
Introduction	9
Inland: high hills and wide valleys	9
Sea cliffs and shorelines	10
Places to stay	11
Getting around	11

The walks

1.	Portpatrick and Dunskey Glen	13
2.	Garlieston to Cruggleton Castle	17
3.	Around Loch Trool	23
4.	Knockman Wood	29
5.	Cally Palace and Temple	33
6.	St Mary's Isle	39
7.	Threave Gardens and Castle	45
8.	The Mulloch and Water of Ken	51
9.	Balcary Point	57
10.	Sandyhills to Rockcliffe	61
11.	Criffel summit	69
12.	Mabie Forest	75
13.	Burns Walk, Dumfries	79
14.	River Annan	85
15.	Langholm and Potholm Hill	89

Useful information 95

USING THIS GUIDE

Routes in this book

In this book you will find a selection of easy or moderate walks suitable for almost everyone, including casual walkers and families with children, or for when you only have a short time to fill. The routes have been carefully chosen to allow you to explore the area and its attractions. Although there may be some climbs there is no challenging terrain, but do bear in mind that conditions can sometimes be wet or muddy underfoot. A route summary table is included on page 6 to help you choose the right walk.

Clothing and footwear

You won't need any special equipment to enjoy these walks. The weather in Britain can be changeable, so choose clothing suitable for the season and wear or carry a waterproof jacket. For footwear, comfortable walking boots or trainers with a good grip are best. A small rucksack for drinks, snacks and spare clothing is useful. See www.adventuresmart.uk.

Walk descriptions

At the beginning of each walk you'll find all the information you need:

- start/finish location, with postcode and a what3words address to help you find it
- parking and transport information, estimated walking time, total distance and climb
- details of public toilets available along the route and where you can get refreshments
- a summary of the key highlights of the walk and what you might see

Timings given are the time to complete the walk at a reasonable walking pace. Allow extra time for extended stops or if walking with children.

The route is described in clear, easy-to-follow directions, with each waypoint marked on an accompanying map extract. It's a good idea to read the whole of the route instructions before setting out, so that you know what to expect.

Maps, GPX files and what3words

Extracts from the OS® 1:25,000 map accompany each route. GPX files for all the walks in this book are available to download at www.cicerone.co.uk/1172/gpx.

What3words is a free smartphone app which identifies every 3m square of the globe with a unique three-word address, e.g. ///destiny.cafe.sonic. For more information see https://what3words.com/products/what3words-app.

USING THIS GUIDE

Walking with children

Even young children can be surprisingly strong walkers, but every family is different and you may need to adapt the timings given in this book to take that into account. Make sure you go at the pace of the slowest member and choose a walk with an exciting objective in mind, such as a cave, river, waterfall or picnic spot. Many of the walks can be shortened to suit – suggestions are included at the end of the route description.

Dogs

Sheep or cattle may be found grazing on a number of these walks. Keep dogs under control at all times so that they don't scare or disturb livestock or wildlife. Cattle, particularly cows with calves, may very occasionally pose a risk to walkers with dogs. If you ever feel threatened by cattle, you should let go of your dog's lead and let it run free.

Enjoying the countryside responsibly

Enjoy the countryside and treat it with respect to protect our natural environments. Stick to footpaths and take your litter home with you. When driving, slow down on rural roads and park considerately, or better still use public transport. For more details check out www.gov.uk/countryside-code.

The Countryside Code

Respect everyone
- be considerate to those living in, working in and enjoying the countryside
- leave gates and property as you find them
- do not block access to gateways or driveways when parking
- be nice, say hello, share the space
- follow local signs and keep to marked paths unless wider access is available

Protect the environment
- take your litter home – leave no trace of your visit
- do not light fires and only have BBQs where signs say you can
- always keep dogs under control and in sight
- dog poo – bag it and bin it – any public waste bin will do
- care for nature – do not cause damage or disturbance

Enjoy the outdoors
- check your route and local conditions
- plan your adventure – know what to expect and what you can do
- enjoy your visit, have fun, make a memory

SHORT WALKS IN DUMFRIES & GALLOWAY

ROUTE SUMMARY TABLE

WALK NAME	START POINT	TIME	DISTANCE
1. Portpatrick and Dunskey Glen	Portpatrick harbour	2hr	5km (3 miles)
2. Garlieston to Cruggleton Castle	Garlieston seafront	4hr	11.5km (7¼ miles)
3. Around Loch Trool	Caldons, Glentrool Forest	3½hr	10km (6¼ miles)
4. Knockman Wood	Knockman Wood, Newton Stewart	2¾hr	7.5km (4¾ miles)
5. Cally Palace and Temple	Gatehouse of Fleet	2½hr	7km (4¼ miles)
6. St Mary's Isle	Kirkcudbright harbour	2½hr	8km (5 miles)
7. Threave Gardens and Castle	Threave Gardens, Castle Douglas	2½hr	6.5km (4 miles)
8. The Mulloch and Water of Ken	St John's Town of Dalry	2hr	5km (3 miles)
9. Balcary Point	South of Auchencairn	2¼hr	5.5km (3½ miles)
10. Sandyhills to Rockcliffe	Sandyhills	3hr	7.5km (4¾ miles)
11. Criffel summit	New Abbey	4½hr	9.5km (6 miles)
12. Mabie Forest	Mabie Forest, Dumfries	3¼hr	8km (5 miles)
13. Burns Walk, Dumfries	Midsteeple, Dumfries	3¼hr	9.5km (6 miles)
14. River Annan	Town Hall, Annan	3¾hr	11km (6¾ miles)
15. Langholm and Potholm Hill	Langholm	3¾hr	9.5km (6 miles)

MAP KEY

HIGHLIGHTS
Cliffs, beach, wooded glen
Gardens, coast, ruined castle
Loch, mountains, battle site
Woodland, wildlife, Bronze Age cairn
Woods, loch, folly
Artists' town, coastline
Gardens, island, castle
Hill with views, river
Clifftops, view of England
Dramatic clifftops, beaches
Viewpoint hill above ancient abbey village
Woodland with tiny loch
Riverside, Robert Burns sites
Riverside and woodlands
River, hill with views

SYMBOLS USED ON ROUTE MAPS

 Start point

 Finish point

 Start and finish at the same place

 Waypoint

 Route line

MAPPING IS SHOWN AT A SCALE OF 1:25,000

```
0 KM      0.25      0.5
|----|----|----|----|
0 miles       0.25
```

DOWNLOADED THE GPX FILES FOR FREE AT
www.cicerone.co.uk/1172/GPX

Criffel granite and Nith estuary (Walk 11)

INTRODUCTION

Portpatrick harbour (Walk 1)

Are you looking for a green and peaceful corner of the UK: one with a chunk of rugged mountain country but also a coastline of rocky coves and golden sandy beaches, along with ancient oakwoods and wide rivers where the salmon run? Somewhere that's out of the way, but at the same time reasonably easy to get to?

Or maybe you already live here in Galloway. In which case you're already well aware of our quiet country roads, our handsome small towns of red sandstone or grey granite, our secret beaches, and our miles and miles of footpaths by riversides and woodlands and along windy cliffs.

Inland: high hills and wide valleys

The interior of Dumfries & Galloway is hilly and rugged. The Merrick (843m) is the highest point in southern Scotland, and the rough heartland around it is known as the Galloway Highlands. Walk 3 at Loch Trool is perfect for looking up at these big hills. Meanwhile Walk 8 in the Glenkens and Walk 15 at Langholm take you up smaller hills – but with big views. And for those up for a tougher challenge, 570m Criffel (Walk 11) is Dumfries's home hill, high above the Solway Firth.

The wide valleys of Eskdale, Annandale, Nithsdale and the Glenkens divide the higher ground. Here are deep green oakwoods, generously watered by the region's rainfall. Yes, you will occasionally be needing a waterproof jacket in Galloway. But that rainfall gathers into the wonderful rivers, wide between their wooded banks, and the same silver-grey as the salmon swimming up them. Walks 8, 13, 14 and 15 feature the Water of Ken, the Nith, the Annan and the Esk respectively.

Almost as wide as the rivers themselves are the open streets of the stone-built towns. Two centuries ago, this was a rich and prosperous landscape, sending tens of thousands of cows southwards into England every autumn. This wealth combined with the easy-to-work red sandstone and classic granite to give rise to the area's handsome high streets. Several of the walks start from the town centres, heading out into the surrounding parkland and woods: Walk 2 out of Garlieston; Walk 4 optionally out of Newton Stewart; Walk 5 from Gatehouse; Walk 6 from Kirkcudbright; Walk 14 from Annan.

Sea cliffs and shorelines

But possibly the greatest glory of Dumfries & Galloway is its coast. Warmed by the Gulf Stream, the shoreline is green and intricate, with palm trees, rocky cliffs and little sandy beaches. Here you look across the Solway's gleaming mudflats or even more shining sea to the blue shadow that is Ireland, or the Isle of Man, or the humped hills of England. Closer at hand you might just spot a porpoise or some seals.

One third of the walks in this guidebook are coastal ones. We start at Portpatrick (Walk 1), the ancient former seaport for Ireland. Walk 2 follows woods and clifftops to one of the book's five ruined castles (not to mention two ruined abbeys and a fortified bastle house). Kirkcudbright's almost-island features on Walk 6, while Walk 9 offers airy clifftops with views across to England. And in the east, the linear walk from Sandyhills to Rockcliffe or Kippford (Walk 10) is well worth catching the early morning bus for.

High on Criffel (Walk 11)

Galloway offers superb coastal walking

Places to stay

For car travellers, the region's former farmworkers' cottages mean that it's very well supplied with self-catering accommodation. But the handsome towns could be even more tempting. Castle Douglas, known as the 'food town', is a lively shopping centre, and has good bus links with almost all the walks in this book. Newton Stewart was formerly famed as having more pubs per head of population than anywhere else in Scotland.

Kirkcudbright is the artists' town, settled back in the 1940s for the sake of its pretty harbour and the clear seaside light. Today the whole region is noted for its artists and craftspeople. The late May holiday weekend sees almost 100 of their studios open to visitors in Spring Fling, Scotland's oldest and biggest such event. Meanwhile in the autumn, lovers of literature will head for Wigtown, Scotland's tiny but official book town.

But perhaps you fancy a seaside village? Portpatrick, Port William and Isle of Whithorn, and further eastwards Kippford and Rockcliffe along with Carsethorn – these are delightful wee places, but you'll need to book your lodgings well in advance.

Getting around

Devorgilla's Bridge over the Nith was built in 1432, and since then Dumfries has been the entry point for Galloway. The town is reached by railway from Carlisle via Annan, or from Glasgow. A good bus service along the A75 links all the main towns and many of the walks in this guidebook. Some coastal walks will need a smaller local bus and a few (such as Loch Trool) are outside the bus network. The Langholm walk (Walk 15) is on the fast bus service between Carlisle and Edinburgh.

Dunskey Castle on the longer route

WALK 1
Portpatrick and Dunskey Glen

Start/finish	*Portpatrick harbour*
Locate	*DG9 8AN ///serves.available.pepper*
Cafes/pubs	*Several pubs at the harbour, golf course clubhouse*
Transport	*Buses from Stranraer*
Parking	*At either end of the harbour*
Toilets	*In car park at north end of harbour (sometimes locked)*

Time 2hr
Distance 5km (3 miles)
Climb 120m

A short but fairly rugged circuit of clifftops, beach and tiny wooded glen

A coastal footpath that is slightly rocky and rugged at one point, a dramatic little glen, and the wide, open spaces of Portpatrick golf course. All this, plus views across the sea to Ireland, make this one of Galloway's finest short coastal walks. You could also use this one just to get to the perfect wee beach at Port Mora, a quiet little cove that's a stiff half-hour walk from the car park.

Portpatrick from the coast path

SHORT WALKS IN DUMFRIES & GALLOWAY

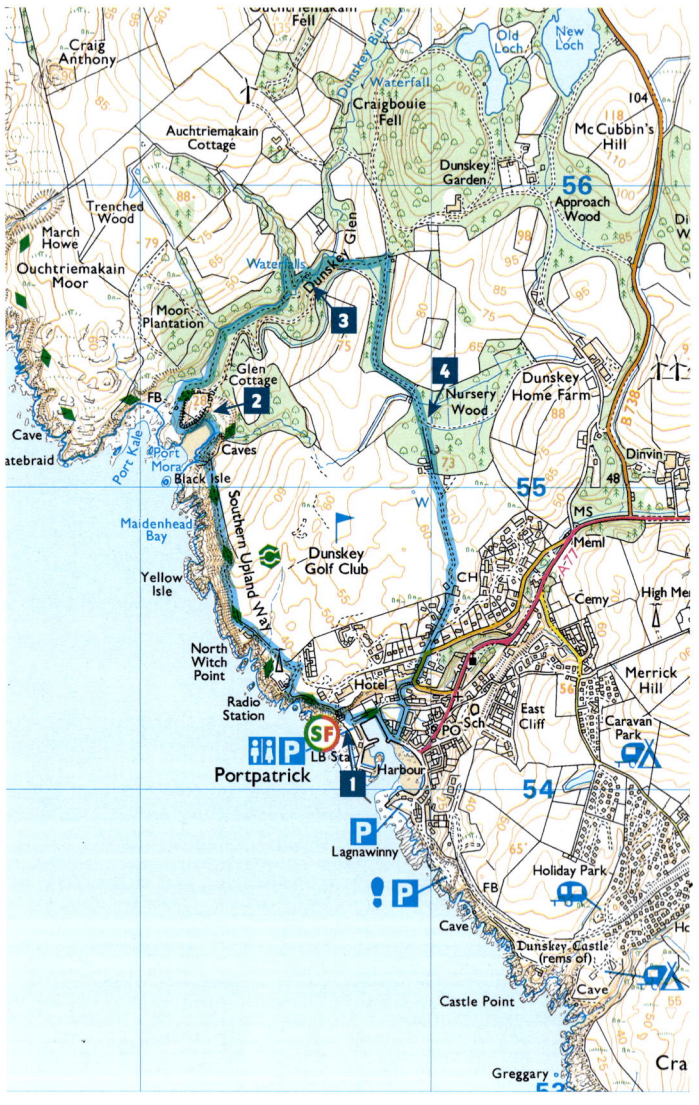

WALK 1 – PORTPATRICK AND DUNSKEY GLEN

Port Kale

1 Start at the north end of the harbour. Concrete steps lead up to the coastal path, marked as the **Southern Upland Way**. A diversion passes to the right of the derelict radio station, then back to the clifftops. After 1km the path drops to the beach at **Port Mora**.

2 At the back of the beach, a wide path leads inland. A few steps up this, turn left on a narrow path round to the shingly **Port Kale**. Just above, a wider but less exciting path leads down to Port Kale, or just stay on the track ahead for the shorter variant. At a path signpost turn inland, forking left into the deep hollow of **Dunskey Glen**. Across a footbridge, the path heads left up a side stream, then doubles back

ⓘ Dumfries & Galloway is one-third the size of Wales. Mull of Galloway to the border of Borders Region takes 2hr 52min by car, according to Viamichelin.

high above the stream to a down-looking viewpoint. In another 100m cross a stone bridge above a waterfall.

3 Once across the bridge turn left, on a path to the right of the stream, to a track beside a woodland cottage. Turn right here, soon passing a track arriving from the right (this is the shorter variant rejoining). At 750m from the woodland cottage a second track forks off right.

SHORT WALKS IN DUMFRIES & GALLOWAY

Signpost at Port Kale

4 Follow this track to a gate out of the woods, and bear left on a track across a **golf course** to its clubhouse. Follow the driveway downhill, keeping ahead at a crossroads. Where the street bends left, steps on the right lead down to a path and a back lane to the harbour.

− To shorten

From Port Mora, you can save a little time (but miss out dramatic Dunskey Glen) by keeping ahead up the track at Waypoint 2 past Glen Cottage. After 1km the woodland track rejoins the main route.

+ To lengthen

From the southern corner of Portpatrick Harbour, just beyond a car park on your right, take a stepped path up left to clifftop level. Continue along a former light railway to the impressive ruins of Dunskey Castle. Return the same way (750m each way, about 40min) and continue the main route.

Portpatrick

The small town takes its name from Ireland's patron saint, which makes sense, given that for many centuries this was the main port for travel across to the other country. Indeed, in the 18th century it was the equivalent of Gretna Green, the landing point for underage couples arriving to exploit more permissive marriage laws of Scotland. In the 1840s Portpatrick lost out to the deeper water port at Stranraer – which, with the coming of large jetfoil ferries to Belfast, was taken over in its turn by Cairnryan.

WALK 2
Garlieston to Cruggleton Castle

Start/finish	*Village hall at Garlieston seafront, just south of Wigtown*
Locate	*DG8 8BQ ///tightest.crowbar.trapdoor*
Cafes/pubs	*Harbour Inn and The Hive cafe at start*
Transport	*Buses from Wigtown and Newton Stewart*
Parking	*Opposite the village hall*
Toilets	*Beside the village hall*

Time 4hr
Distance 11.5km (7¼ miles)
Climb 50m

A longer coastal walk on good paths to a ruined castle

This long, but almost level, walk takes in the planned village of Garlieston, the woodland gardens of Galloway House and the sandy shores of Rigg Bay. But the striking high-point is the single massive arch of Cruggleton Castle. It makes a breezy picnic place and a grand frame for views up and down the Machars coast.

Rigg Bay

WALK 2 – GARLIESTON TO CRUGGLETON CASTLE

Seafront cottages at Garlieston

> ⓘ *Garlieston's pier was built in the 1810s. A busy port in that century, it still has a few boats fishing for whelk and lobster.*

1 From the village hall return along the seafront cottages, then turn left on the main road, signed to Newton Stewart. At the village edge, just before a crossroads, a short path on the left short-cuts onto the estate road running south. Follow this for 1km.

2 With **Galloway House** seen on the left, bear right. The small car park for Galloway House Gardens is on the left, then the track enters woods. After a gate, the wide path bends left to picnic tables at **Rigg Bay**.

At low tide the remains of one of the Mulberry Harbours from WW2 are visible offshore at Rigg Bay. More remains can be seen on the shoreline north of Garlieston, on the path past Eggerness Point. These were the secret trial versions for two 'flat-pack' harbours that were towed across to the Normandy beaches after D-Day. One was destroyed by a storm but the other was successfully used for 10 months, landing millions of tonnes of war supplies.

3 Turn right and continue close to the shoreline through a narrow strip of woodland. The path here is slightly different from the OS map. At **Sliddery Point**, the path heads

Cruggleton Castle

slightly uphill towards the top edge of the wood, then drops again to the wood edge at a stone house. The path passes along some battlements above the cliffs and through an arch to clifftops. After a small gate, follow field edges above the sea to the remnant of **Cruggleton Castle**.

A single free-standing arch is all that remains of the castle. The castle's eventful history starts in the Iron Age, and includes being besieged and captured twice during the Scottish Wars of Independence. In 1563, English spies reported to Queen Elizabeth that it was in good shape, with a tower, surrounding curtain wall and drawbridge with portcullis.

ⓘ *Whithorn, on the Machars peninsular, is the cradle of Christianity in Britain. St Ninian landed here in AD397.*

4 Return to the house at the wood edge. Continue into the woods for 20m, then head back left through open woodland to join the track beyond the house. The track leads through parkland fields for 1.5km to join a minor road (B7063) where you turn right. After 400m, as the road bends left, squeeze through a gap alongside a field gate on the right and follow a track towards the sea along the right-hand edge of a field. After 300m, a side track joins from the right and an old iron gate is ahead.

WALK 2 – GARLIESTON TO CRUGGLETON CASTLE

5 Go through the gate into woodland. This is the corner of Galloway House Gardens. Go past a ruin to join a more used path. Turning right along the path here would lead back to the shoreline. Keep ahead, then with a gate into open fields ahead the path bends right, then bends back left again. It runs to the right of a wall to join the wide path coming up from the shoreline picnic tables. Follow it ahead and into the gardens' car park.

A little shelter has a map of the woodland gardens, which feature snowdrops, daffodils, rhododendrons and a celebrated handkerchief tree that flowers in late spring.

6 From the car park enter the woodlands and take the path to the left. It bends right near **Galloway House**. Now keep ahead on any path to the shoreline. Turn left towards Garlieston on the clear path along the shoreline, through woods then beside salt meadows and the wide foreshore. You reach the village edge at the old stone **pier**, with the village hall just ahead.

– To shorten

Start at the car park for Galloway House Gardens (Waypoint 6) and go through the gardens to the shore. Turn right past Rigg Bay to Cruggleton Castle and follow the main walk from there back to the gardens (7.5km, 2hr 40min).

Fishing boats at Garlieston harbour

21

Foot of Loch Trool

WALK 3
Around Loch Trool

Time 3½hr
Distance 10km (6¼ miles)
Climb 150m

A circuit of the wooded loch on good, clear paths

Start/finish	*Forestry Commission car park at Caldons, near Glentrool Village*
Locate	*DG8 6SU ///meanings.parting.fruitcake*
Cafes/pubs	*None on route*
Transport	*Occasional buses to Glentrool village*
Parking	*At start, and at Bruce's Stone. May fill up at busy holiday periods*
Toilets	*No public toilets on route*

A smooth, well-made path runs right around southern Scotland's most beautiful loch. There are views up to the magnificent Merrick hills, and ancient oakwoods to walk under. But for enthusiasts of Scottish Independence all this is of small significance compared to the crucial Battle of Glentrool, where Robert the Bruce and his fighters ambushed forces loyal to the English king.

Loch Trool seen from up in the hills

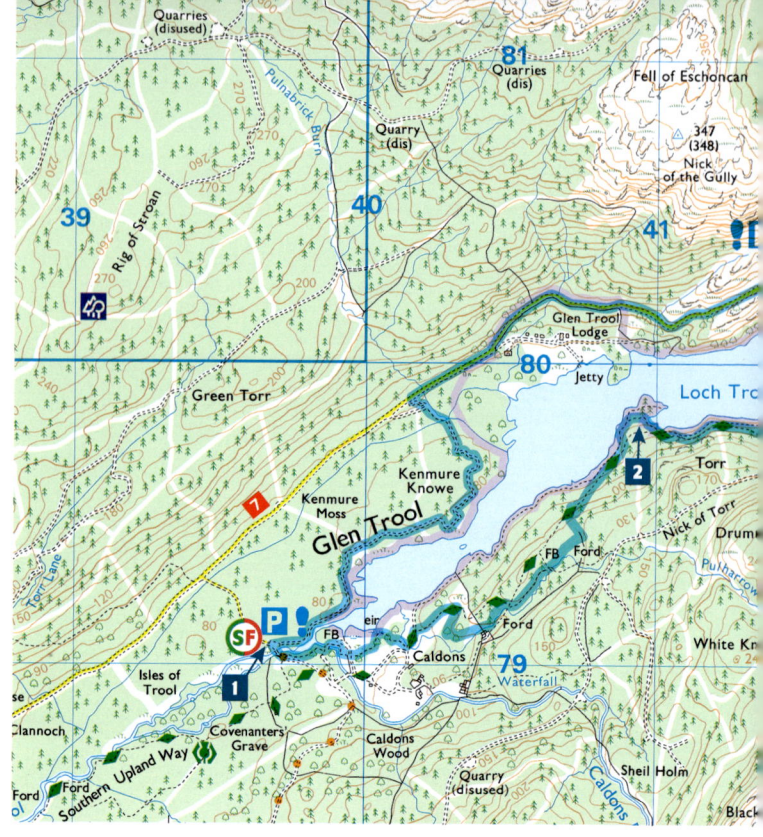

1 From the car park, the track continues across **Water of Trool**, the outflow stream from Loch Trool. At once turn left on a wide, well-made path. After a footbridge and a glimpse of Loch Trool the path meets a wider track. Turn left here. After crossing a stream, keep to the main path that bends up to the right. Soon it contours among mature Scots Pines, then works down to a bay of **Loch Trool**.

> ⓘ *Galloway Forest Park is one of only four in Scotland. The others are Tay, Tweed Valley and the Queen Elizabeth Forest Park (Trossachs).*

2 The pinewood promontory on the left is a viewpoint and picnic place. Follow the main path, which continues along the wooded slope above the

Beside Loch Trool

SHORT WALKS IN DUMFRIES & GALLOWAY

Bruce's Stone

loch. After clear felling in the 2010s, birch is competing with larch to take over this slope. As you pass through the ambush site, a noticeboard describes the Battle of Glentrool. The path climbs steeply above the head of the loch, then slants downhill to meet the Glenhead Burn. Head upstream for 200m to a track bridge.

3 Turn left, across the burn, and follow the track back through ancient oakwoods. After 600m you cross the small cataract of **Gairland Burn**. In another 750m, after the stone Buchan Bridge, the track climbs quite steeply. Where it bends right, take a rough path up left that leads directly to **Bruce's Stone**, raised high above Loch Trool. Alternatively, you can follow the track to the car park at its top and turn left to the stone.

4 A wide path heads away from Bruce's Stone to a car park. Turn left down the small tarmac road, passing

> ⓘ *At 843m, The Merrick in Galloway Forest Park is the highest point between England and the Scottish Highlands.*

WALK 3 – AROUND LOCH TROOL

The Battle of Glentrool

During the turbulent beginning of the 14th century, Robert the Bruce, one of several claimants to the Scottish crown, held out in the Galloway Hills with a small band of guerrilla fighters. Here at Loch Trool, in 1307, they ambushed a larger force loyal to King Edward II of England, first rolling down boulders from the slopes of Mulldonoch then leaping down through the trees with their broadswords. Bruce's Stone on the opposite shore is supposed to be where the future king stood to direct the battle – presumably using signal flags or a trumpet. This first small victory led to growing support, and eventually, seven years later, to the final defeat of the English at Bannockburn.

Footpath signpost for Loch Trool trail

through a second car park. After 800m the road descends quite steeply, to pass the driveway end of **Glen Trool Lodge**. In another 400m, turn left at a path signpost onto a wide, smooth path. This runs through scrubby woodland with glimpses of the loch, then beside Water of Trool for the last few steps to the car park.

Knockman Wood

WALK 4
Knockman Wood

Time 2¾hr
Distance 7.5km (4¾ miles)
Climb 150m

An atmospheric walk through ancient woodland and even more ancient remains

Start/finish	Knockman Wood, Minnigaff, north of Newton Stewart
Locate	DG8 6SL ///usual.midwinter.interacts
Cafes/pubs	Pubs and cafes in Newton Stewart
Transport	Buses to Newton Stewart from Dumfries
Parking	Walker's car park at Knockman Wood (fork left after Minnigaff Church and take the third driveway on the right, through a gateway with a 'core path' signpost)
Toilets	Riverside car park, Newton Stewart

Well-made paths lead through beautiful open woodland, with wildlife from barn owls to bluebells, and clearings giving views up to Cairnsmore of Fleet. The oak trees could be 500 years old, about the same age as the farm settlement at Pheasant Liggat, with its intriguing corn kiln explained by interpretation boards on site. But roughly six times as ancient as these is the Bronze Age cairn at the turning point of the walk.

Chambered cairn in Knockman Wood

1 If you've arrived by bus in Newton Stewart, head north along the A714 (Girvan) and bear right to a footbridge over the River Cree. Cross to a riverside path on the left and follow the directions from Waypoint 6 to the car park in Knockman Wood. Starting from the walker's car park in **Knockman Wood**, check its paths map: the route described here will follow yellow then white trails (but be aware that the waymark colours of official trails sometimes change). Turn right (north) and at once fork left around a locked gate. In 800m, as the track bends right, take a wide, waymarked path ahead.

Corn kiln at Pheasant Liggat

2 The path crosses a track. For a short diversion follow the marker for the blue trail on the right for 200m to a dragonfly pool. The main path continues ahead for 1km, where the huge, sprawling **chambered cairn** is seen on the left.

> The cairn is around 6000 years old. Charred human remains have been found inside similar ones, which are quite common around here. The internal chamber has collapsed, but two large 'orthostats', doorposts, remain.

3 The main path bends to the right, roughly level then winding downhill to a clearing with a well-built wall below. It passes the pit that is the former corn kiln, then bends left through the wall and between the remains of the settlement at **Pheasant Liggat**. This 'fermtoun', or farm settlement, is probably medieval. Remains of several homesteads lie among the bracken.

4 Just below the fermtoun, where the waymarked path bends right at the corner of a plantation, take a farm gate on the left. A green track leads across moorland to a junction with a solitary thorn tree. Turn left here to lengthen the walk to Garlies Castle.

> ⓘ *Newton Stewart and Minnigaff, on opposite sides of River Cree, were once two different towns in different counties, separated by a tricky ford.*

Penkiln Burn

5 Turn right down the track, which soon joins a smooth gravel track alongside Penkiln Burn. Follow this downstream; it shortcuts away from the burn then rejoins it to the edge of Minnigaff. Cross **Queen Mary's Bridge** on your left and take the lane into **Minnigaff**. After 800m, turn back right across Penkiln Burn.

6 A path above the river leads into the kirkyard of Minnigaff **church**. Pass around it to rejoin the lane. Fork left and follow the lane for 500m to the start of woodland, then take the third driveway on the right, with a footpath sign. The forest track leads back to the walker's car park.

− To shorten

From Waypoint 4, the wide main path leads directly back to the walker's car park in 1km (giving a total walk of 4.5km with 120m climb, about 1hr 45min).

+ To lengthen

From Waypoint 5, the track left leads in 1.2km to the ruined Garlies Castle. A 200m stretch of the track is very damp and mucky, especially in winter (adds 2.5km and 1hr to the walk).

WALK 5
Cally Palace and Temple

Start/finish	Fleet Bridge at the centre of Gatehouse of Fleet
Locate	DG7 2JP ///boater.joys.uncle
Cafes/pubs	Pubs and cafes in Gatehouse, and Cally Palace Hotel
Transport	Buses from Dumfries
Parking	Car park in town centre, or Cally Woods car park (join route at Waypoint 7)
Toilets	In town centre car park

Time 2½hr
Distance 7km (4¼ miles)
Climb 70m

A woodland walk to a temple that's a must for lovers of the slightly odd

This woodland walk starts from the attractive granite town of Gatehouse of Fleet, a former port. The Cally Estate has various ornamental features from the early 19th century – a lake, a folly tower, plus the Cally Palace itself, now a hotel. All this is folded away in mature woodland of beech and oak.

Cally Lake

SHORT WALKS IN DUMFRIES & GALLOWAY

WALK 5 – CALLY PALACE AND TEMPLE

Masonic Arms in Gatehouse of Fleet

1 Head east along the High Street to the nearby town centre car park. At its back, a footpath sign points to the right. The wide path winds through woodland, until a faux Georgian bridge on the right leads onto the edge of a golf course. The pele tower, Cardoness Castle, can be seen in the distance.

2 Turn left on a wide path alongside the wood, continuing just inside it. Look out for the remains of Cally Castle on your right. As the path emerges again onto open golf course, the Cally Palace is seen ahead. At this point you can carefully head left across the golf course to the corner of **Cally Lake**. Continue to the tarmac driveway in front of the **Cally Palace Hotel**.

3 Turn right on the tarmac lane, soon passing under the **A75** road. After a brick house, take the track left that is marked as Bike Path 7.

4 Continue along this forest track. It wanders close to the noisy A75, then away again to a junction. Here turn left, still marked as Bike Path 7, to cross a low stone bridge. In another 50m, turn left to the Temple.

5 Pass to the right of **the Temple**, onto a path continuing to a junction with an interpretation board. Turn left, on a path which runs alongside the noisy road, then passes underneath it. The path leads away from the road to a junction with a faded yellow-trail waymarker.

The Temple

6 Turn right on a wide path wandering through woodland to meet a track. Here turn left, soon with open field on the right. After re-entering woodland, a waymarker on the left marks your path on the right. In a few steps fork left to cross a footbridge and pass under the tall beech trees of **Galla Hill Wood**. If you lose the path here, just drop left to the track. The path drops left to rejoin the track. Continue to a junction with a tarmac driveway.

Rosnes Bench sculpture

Up to the right as you pass through the beechwood are three sculptural benches, made of resin and powdered rock. They are part of a Galloway-wide project called 'Rosnes Benches'.

7 Cross the tarmac driveway to continue ahead, marked 'Link Road'. The track becomes a lane into **Gatehouse**, arriving under the clock tower. Here turn left down the High Street to the main car park and Fleet Bridge.

– To shorten

At the Cally Palace Hotel (Waypoint 3) turn left up the tarmac driveway, to reach Waypoint 7, where you turn left into Gatehouse (4km, about 1hr 15min).

A designed landscape

In 1816 Alexander Murray of Broughton and his new wife set up home in what is now the Cally Palace Hotel, which dates from the 1760s. Their fashionable landscaping included the ornamental lake and the many stone bridges and handsome granite walls. The so-called Temple was designed in the 19th century as a focal feature of views from the house, as well as being a viewpoint itself. In the 1930s the Forestry Commission planted most of the parkland with broadleaf trees; the mature beechwoods towards the end of the walk are especially atmospheric.

At Paul Jones's Point

WALK 6
St Mary's Isle

Start/finish	*Kirkcudbright harbour*
Locate	*DG6 4HY ///scorching.worker.scuba*
Cafes/pubs	*Pubs and cafes in Kirkcudbright centre*
Transport	*Buses from Dumfries*
Parking	*Large car park at the harbour*
Toilets	*At the harbour*

Time 2½hr
Distance 8km (5 miles)
Climb 0m

A woodland and coastal stroll from the historic Artists' Town

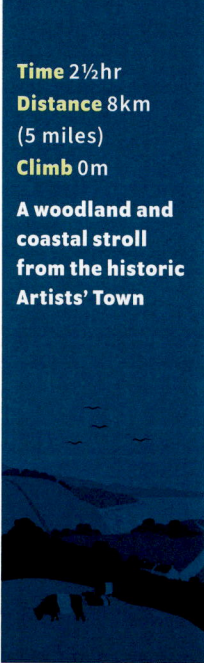

Gentle woodland paths lead around the edge of St Mary's Isle, which isn't actually an island at all. Instead it's a narrow peninsular between the estuary of the River Dee and the tidal flats of Manxman's Bay. The walk starts and ends in the ancient, picturesque town of Kircudbright, a favoured settlement for artists in the early 20th century. But on the way around there are plenty of spots on the lonely foreshore where it's just you, the sea and your sandwiches.

Kirkcudbright harbour

MacLellan's Castle, Kirkcudbright

1 Start by heading downstream, passing to the left of the Harbour Cottage Gallery and right of MacLellan's Castle to curve left into High Street. In 50m, take an alleyway on the right next to Broughton House and go past the entrance to its garden to reach the yacht marina. Broughton House garden is well worth visiting, small but packed with interest.

2 Turn left, downstream, and follow Castledykes Road ahead. Where it bends left, keep ahead on a tarmac path across **Gartshore Park**. This crosses a tarmac track to run beside the earthworks of the older castle at Castledykes. You could dodge out right to enjoy the foreshore here. When the path rejoins Castledykes Road, keep ahead along the road. Soon it bends left through houses towards the **A711**. Immediately before the main road, join a tarmac track on the right, signed as 'St Mary's Isle Circuit'.

3 Follow the track under trees, bearing left past **Great Cross** house. Where the track runs close to the estuary, look out for a path forking off to the right, marked with a waymark post and a painted arrow on a tree.

4 The path runs through open woodland alongside the estuary, with access to the foreshore at several points. As you bend left approaching **Paul Jones's Point**, the ground is scrubby birch and the path is rather overgrown.

Continue to follow the path north, with an exotic bamboo thicket just before it joins an earth track.

5 Keep ahead on this track, through open woodland, ignoring two tracks on the left. After 1.5km it runs out onto the A711 at the edge of **Kirkcudbright**. Turn left on the pavement, passing the end of Castledykes Road towards the town centre and High Street.

> Kirkcudbright's former importance as a port is reflected in various old buildings passed in the High Street on the way to the castle. The Tollbooth, built in the 1620s, was the town hall, sheriff court and prison and still features a set of 'jougs', a metal collar for prisoners. It is now a Council-run art gallery, with free admission.

6 Turn left into High Street (signed for the Selkirk Arms). This bends right at the Tollbooth and passes the ancient Custom House (on your right) to return you to the harbour.

— To shorten

At Waypoint 3 keep ahead to the main road and turn left to rejoin the walk at Waypoint 6, for a 2.5km circuit taking in the town's galleries and historic buildings (about 1hr).

ⓘ Gallovidian John Paul Jones became the first admiral of the US Navy. His ships mounted raids on Whitehaven in England, and Kirkcudbright.

River Dee foreshore, St Mary's Isle

'Kirkcudbright' by John Peploe, Kirkcudbright Gallery

Kirkcudbright

The town's name means 'St Cuthbert's chapel': the saint's corpse paid a brief visit here in its wanderings after the Viking raids on Lindisfarne. An even briefer visitor was local sailor John Paul Jones, who became admiral of the American Navy and raided Kirkcudbright in 1778. The town remains popular for a short stop-over today, as the numerous B&Bs and cafes can testify.

In the years before WW1 the town became renowned as an artists' colony, the picturesque old buildings and harbour attracting painters from the movement called the Glasgow Boys. Examples of their work can be seen in the art gallery on the A711 opposite St Cuthbert's Church.

Threave Castle

WALK 7
Threave Gardens and Castle

Time 2½hr
Distance 6.5km (4 miles)
Climb 80m

A castle view, a garden, an island bird hide and the smallest hill you ever climbed

Start/finish	North edge of Threave Gardens, Castle Douglas
Locate	DG7 1RY ///passages.untruth.models
Cafes/pubs	Cafe at Threave Gardens entrance
Transport	Buses from Castle Douglas and Dumfries stop at Hightae Farm near Waypoint 2
Parking	Car park north of Threave Gardens, or at main car park (turn left at bottom of car park to walk start)
Toilets	At entrance to Threave Gardens and at Kelton Mains farmhouse (Waypoint 3)

This walk through the National Trust for Scotland's Threave Estate just outside Castle Douglas is a great one for bird watchers, with hides overlooking marshland pools, and ospreys on camera at Kelton Mains farmhouse. It's grand, too, for the rest of us, with a big river to enjoy and a view across it to a castle on an island. (Note that Historic Scotland has suspended visits to the castle itself after a safety inspection in 2022.) Garden lovers can, for a modest entrance charge, include the nearby Threave Gardens at either the start or the end of the walk.

Port Hill above River Dee

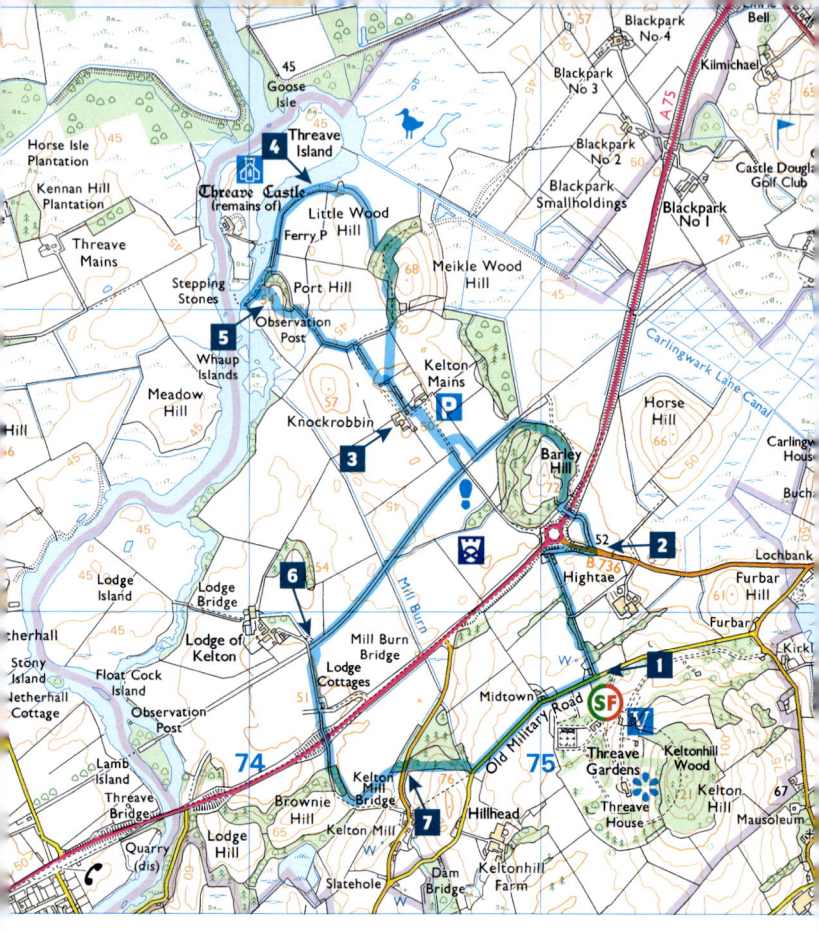

1 From the end of the car park, take the path on the right that runs through trees to cross the nearby road. The path continues to the left of a farm track, then to the right of it. With the A75 road ahead, take a lane on the right, then a path alongside the **B736** briefly, before dropping to cross the road.

2 Take the tarmac track ahead, which crosses above the A75. Turn right for a woodland path around the base of **Barley Hill** to meet the smooth gravelled path of the former south coast railway. Turn left for 300m, then turn right on a gravel path across grass to **Kelton Mains**.

WALK 7 – THREAVE GARDENS AND CASTLE

3 To the left of the main building, turn right on a gravel path to the left of a wall. At the field end bear right on a grass path diagonally across a field to a gate into woodland. Follow the woodland path north for 300m to a junction. A bird hide is ahead here. Take the path down sharp left, out of the wood and over a ditch, then turn right to reach the River Dee opposite **Threave island**.

> Overwintering geese and other water birds can be seen from the various bird hides. Meanwhile in summer the nesting ospreys can be watched via a webcam at Kelton Mains and from the viewing platform near Threave Castle.

4 Take the good path that runs alongside the river, past the osprey observatory viewpoint and then past Threave Castle seen across the water. In another 150m keep ahead alongside the river to Steppingstones Hide. Turn back here, forking up right on a grass path onto the tiny **Port Hill**. This hill has views over the river out of all proportion to its 54m altitude.

5 From Port Hill the path runs down to join a wide grassy path away from the river, soon on raised duckboards above a boggy wetland area. Turn right, then take a path on the left past a bench to rejoin your outward walk. The gravel path bends right, back to **Kelton Mains**. Head back out towards the railway but stay on the access track. Before the bridge where this track crosses the railway, a gate on the right leads to an overgrown little path down to the railway track. Continue to the right, mostly in a cutting, for 800m to meet a tarmac lane. Here if time allows you could continue ahead to visit Lamb Island.

Path beside River Dee

6 Turn left on the tarmac lane (signposted for Bridge of Ken), then keep ahead onto a track to re-cross the **A75**. In another 150m, on entering a wood, turn left on a path along the wood's edge. After a footbridge, the path runs through fields and woods to a minor road.

7 Cross the road to a woodland path, which runs to join the even smaller **Old Military Road**. Cross and turn left into the footpath that runs alongside the road. After 500m turn right into the car park at the walk start. To visit Threave Gardens, walk to the car park entrance, but before you reach the road turn off right, and pass round to the left of a fenced enclosure.

Cows near Kelton Mill

WALK 7 – THREAVE GARDENS AND CASTLE

Garden of Contemplation, Threave Gardens

− To shorten
Start and end at the small car park at Kelton Mains (Waypoint 3) for a short riverside walk (gives a total walk of 2.5km, 1hr).

+ To lengthen
From Waypoint 6 continue ahead along the old railway to Lamb Island and the bird hide at its upstream end (adds 1.5km, 30min).

Threave Gardens

The garden alongside the walk start (small entrance charge) is one of Galloway's finest, run by the National Trust for Scotland. It's used for training horticultural students, and the various 'garden rooms' are in a rich variety of styles. Odd-looking ornamental grasses are one of its specialities. The walled garden and glasshouses are a more obvious attraction, especially the magnificent tree ferns. The woodland garden features snowdrops, bluebells and red squirrels. But do also consult a garden map to find the tiny, hidden jewel that is the 'Garden of Contemplation' – looking out to the surrounding countryside, and as much sculpture as garden, it was built as a memorial of the Lockerbie aeroplane disaster of 1988.

Heading down towards Water of Ken

WALK 8
The Mulloch and Water of Ken

Time 2hr
Distance 5km (3 miles)
Climb 120m

A modest hill with big views and a quiet riverside return

Start/finish	Clachan Inn, St John's Town of Dalry
Locate	DG7 3SW ///improvise.audible.modern
Cafes/pubs	Pubs and cafes at start
Transport	Buses from Castle Douglas, several daily
Parking	In main street or at Waypoint 4
Toilets	Behind the town hall in Dalry

This walk offers a small hill above Dalry, but one with great views of the Galloway Hills. The return leg is alongside the wide River Ken. Combine this with a walker-friendly pub on what is both an ancient pilgrim route to Whithorn and today's Southern Upland Way, and you're onto a winner.

Main Street, Dalry

1 From the Clachan Inn head up the village street until it levels. Turn back sharp right into Kirkland St, then in 80m left up a tarmac lane signed as 'Watson Bird Walk'. The lane becomes a farm track, then a faint grass one up towards Mulloch Hill.

2 Ignore a gate ahead but turn up left, the track now very faint. It bends right below a fence. Keep ahead through a field gate with a small walker's gate inset, then take another such gate on your left. Head back to the right across this field, aiming for the hilltop. Another multi-access gate leads onto the summit hump of **Mulloch Hill**, with signpost, trig point and wide views.

3 Keep ahead to a wall and follow it downhill, soon passing through it by a gate, then back again by a gate lower down. When confronted by gorse bushes, ease away from the wall to

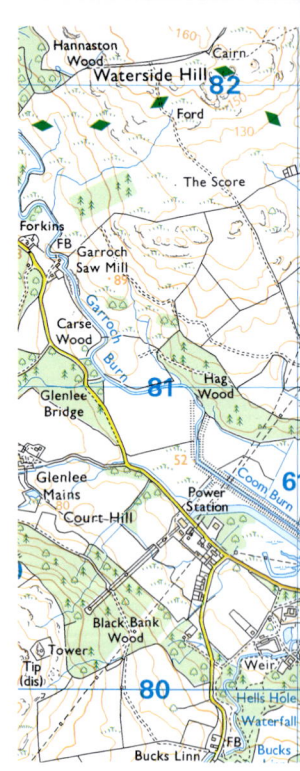

WALK 8 – THE MULLOCH AND WATER OF KEN

Riverside path near Dalry

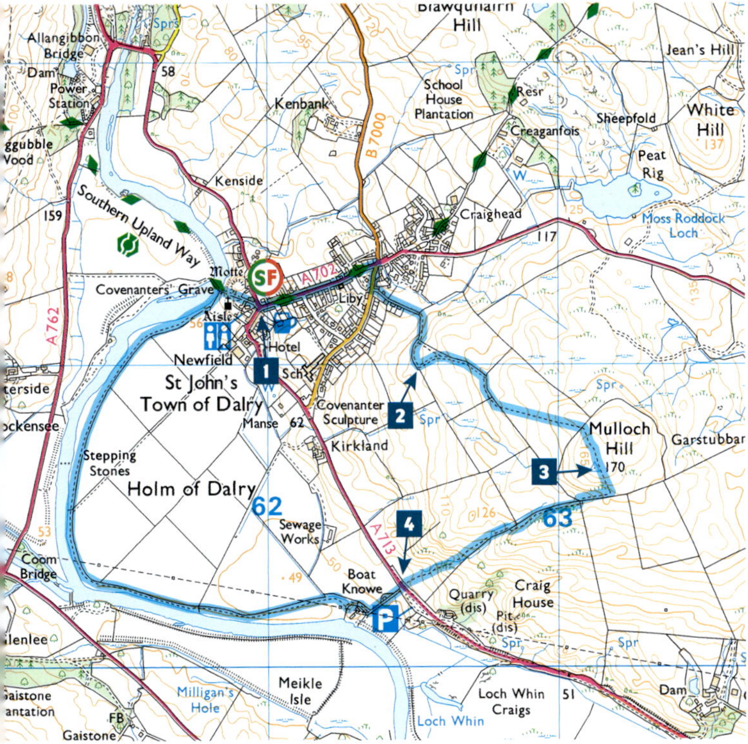

Southern Upland Way footbridge

follow a stream trickle down to a hidden gate onto the **A713**. A car park lay-by is just to the left, the alternative start point.

4 Cross into the driveway of **Boat Knowe**. Before the house turn right to a path along the flood bank beside the Water of Ken. You can also walk closer beside the big river. After 1km you pass the tailrace of Glenlee hydropower station gushing into the river and in another 1km you reach the high footbridge used by the **Southern Upland Way**. Cross this if you want to wander onwards towards Waterside Hill. Turn up steps away from the footbridge. On your right now is a stile into the kirkyard if you want to visit the Covenanter's Grave. Otherwise keep ahead up to the village street at the walk start.

> ⓘ *The years 1679–88 in Galloway are known as the Killing Times, as Presbyterian Protestants were persecuted by the government of the Stuart kings.*

> **＋ To lengthen**
>
> Continue over the Southern Upland Way (SU) footbridge and head upstream along the riverbank. Follow SU Way markers across the A762 to a saddle on Waterside Hill and turn right across humpy ground to the summit cairn. The out-and-back route is 3km with 100m of climb, adding 1hr 30min to the walk.

The Dalry Uprising

Covenanters' Grave at Dalry church

In the kirkyard in St John's Town of Dalry you will find the Covenanters' Grave, a table-type tomb memorial to martyred Presbyterian Protestants who were opposed to state-sanctioned bishops and ministers. In the Dalry Uprising of 1666, some of these local Covenanters marched towards Edinburgh in armed rebellion against the King and Scottish Government. The hopeless attempt was crushed at a small battle in the Pentland Hills. Details are on interpretation boards outside and (if open) inside the town hall.

Lot's Wife sea stack

WALK 9
Balcary Point

Time 2¼hr
Distance 5.5km (3½ miles)
Climb 100m

A wild coastal circuit with a section above high cliffs and views across to England

Start/finish	Lane end south of Auchencairn
Locate	DG7 1QZ ///dearest.safety.roosters
Cafes/pubs	Balcary Bay Hotel at start
Transport	No public transport
Parking	Car park at lane end
Toilets	None unless using the hotel

This airy clifftop walk has sea stacks to look down at, sheltered pebbly beaches to play about on, and (on a clear day) views across the Solway to the hills of the Lake District. It's especially rewarding in the off-season when those views are even clearer and the clifftops are quieter. The path runs across sloping ground immediately above the cliffs, so may be unsuitable for the nervous, as well as uncontrolled dogs or children.

Above Airds Point

SHORT WALKS IN DUMFRIES & GALLOWAY

> ⓘ *Robin Rigg, with 60 turbines, was Scotland's first offshore windfarm. But its electricity all goes into England.*

1 Start at the far end of the car park, where a woodland path leads into an open field. Here a path on the right heads across fields to bypass the high clifftops. Cross the left edge of the field, to a kissing gate onto a woodland path. This suddenly emerges onto clifftops above **Balcary Point**.

2 The path runs below a fence above **Lot's Wife** sea stack and along the clifftops (if conditions are slippery, you could cross the fence into the field alongside). The high clifftop

Above Balcary Point

WALK 9 – BALCARY POINT

section ends at a small gate next to the cliff edge. Here the shortcut route turns back inland.

> Just as many sea arches are named the Needle's Eye, sea stacks tend to commemorate Lot's Wife. In the Book of Genesis, God plans to destroy the wicked city of Sodom with fire and brimstone. He instructs Lot to flee with all his family, without looking back at the destruction. Lot's wife, the one who does look back, is turned into a pillar of salt.

3 Continue along more open clifftops, passing above Airds Point. After 1km the path drops to the shoreline. In another 500m, pass along behind a row of beach shacks, to find a green track running inland.

> ⓘ *Robin Rigg's wind turbines are 125m high including blades, and stand in 35m of water, with foundations 35m into the sea bed.*

59

View towards Rascarrel Bay

If you are very lucky you could catch a glimpse of harbour porpoises from this clifftop. They are smaller than dolphins, and the sickle-shaped dorsal fin is towards the back of their bodies rather than in the middle. It's a long shot, but bring the binoculars just in case.

4 The track runs to the corner of **Loch Mackie**. Just through a gate, turn right, away from the loch, with a wall to your right. The earth track gets clearer as it runs through fields to the car park.

− To shorten
From Waypoint 3, turn right through a small walker's gate, to head inland to the right of a wall. After a gate, as the track ahead bends left, bear right (waymarked) to the corner of a hedge. Follow this ahead to a gate into a walled path. At its end, turn left to the nearby car park (2.5km, about 1hr).

+ To lengthen
From Waypoint 4, a track continues along the shore to Rascarrel Bay, where it turns inland to meet a minor road. Turn right for 600m then take a track on the right. After 400m a path forking right leads through rough scrubby woods to Loch Mackie, where you rejoin the main route (gives a total walk of 8km, about 3hr).

WALK 10
Sandyhills to Rockcliffe

Time 3hr
Distance 7.5km (4¾ miles)
Climb 200m

A linear walk along the area's most spectacular clifftops

Start	*Bus interchange at Sandyhills beach*
Locate	*DG5 4NY ///bandaged.richly.corn*
Finish	*Bus stop at road end in Rockcliffe*
Cafes/pubs	*Cafe and two pubs at Kippford on longer route*
Transport	*Buses from Dumfries to Sandyhills via New Abbey, and from Rockcliffe and Kippford to Dalbeattie for Dumfries*
Parking	*Pay & display car park at start, or park at Rockcliffe for 2-hourly bus to Sandyhills*
Toilets	*At start and Rockcliffe*

This fairly strenuous clifftop walk looks out across the wide tidal sands and the Solway to the Lake District hills. There's a wild rocky foreshore and several secret beaches along the way – all in all well worth the bother of the bus link from Rockcliffe for car drivers. Meanwhile those travelling by bus enjoy a circular tour from Dumfries, out via New Abbey, then Dalbeattie on the way back.

Warning sign at Sandyhills

1 Pass round to the left of the parking area, for a boardwalk onto the beach. Turn right along the back of the beach to cross a substantial footbridge over **Barnhourie Burn**.

> The sandy beach runs down to the enormous Mersehead Sands. Wandering out on the sandbanks is risky, as the channel of Southwick Water can fill on the incoming tide behind you, cutting you off.

2 Fork right, passing path signposts, to where the path starts uphill. A last side-path on the left leads to a charming little beach. The path is rugged and pretty steep, then levels along an open field where there is a glimpse down to the sea arch **Needles Eye**. The path rises across the flank of **Torrs Hill**, then gradually downhill, beside the clifftop walls, to a lane foot at Portling. The steep track down left leads to Portling Bay.

3 Turn up right on the rough unsurfaced lane into **High Portling**. At a T-junction turn left along a lane. Before the final houses, a signpost marks a path on the right, slanting up the steep flank of **White Hill** between gorse bushes. The path then descends on field edges. After a gate, it runs above the foreshore, to the left of fences and walls. In 600m there's a path junction above a stone cairn at **Bells Isle**.

Approaching Portling

WALK 10 – SANDYHILLS TO ROCKCLIFFE

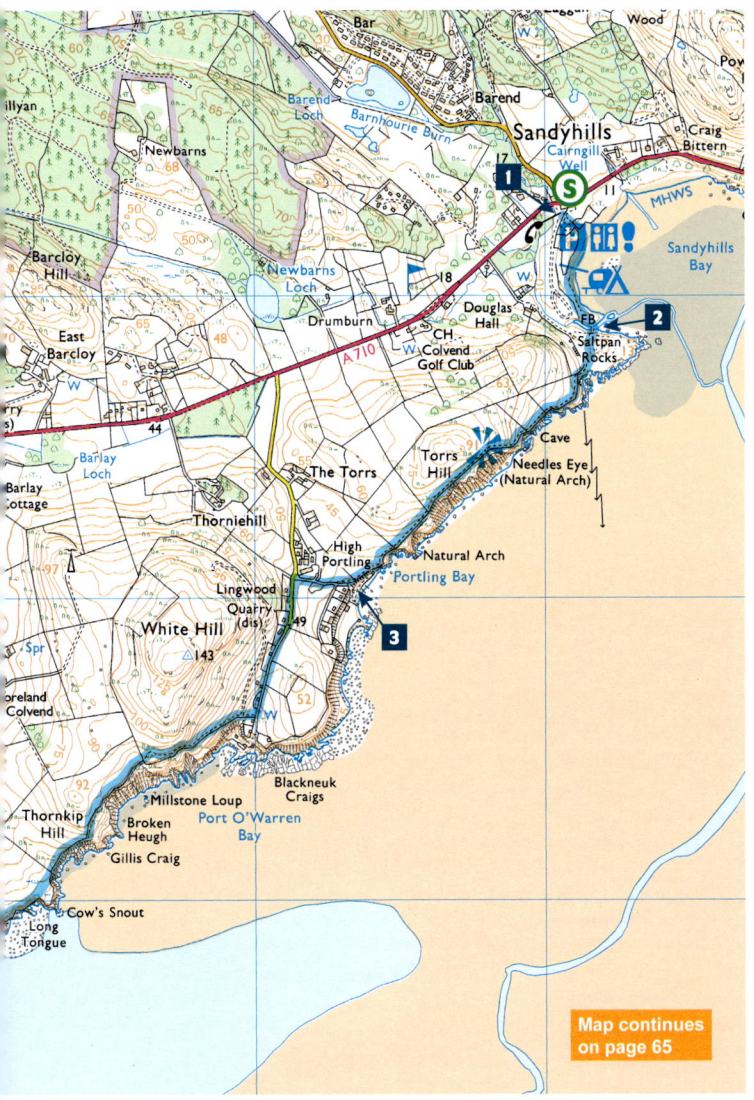

Map continues on page 65

SHORT WALKS IN DUMFRIES & GALLOWAY

64

WALK 10 – SANDYHILLS TO ROCKCLIFFE

Clifftops at Elbe memorial

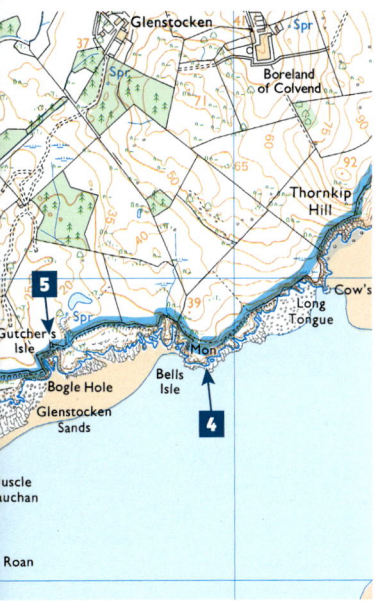

4 The cairn below the path commemorates the wreck of the Elbe. The Elbe was wrecked in a storm in December 1867. Everyone on board managed to scramble ashore here. The main shoreline path next passes a ruin above **Gutcher's Isle**.

The ruin was a bastle, or fortified farmhouse, abandoned in Victorian times. The little beach below makes a grand place to explore, especially with children. The 'Isle' is a rock stack with narrow channels either side. There's no sign of the hermit who once lived on top of it.

5 The path continues above the rocky shoreline for another 500m, then

WALK 10 – SANDYHILLS TO ROCKCLIFFE

Rockcliffe bay

climbs up the flank of **Barcloy Hill**. It levels off, then slants down to open fields. A steep path down left would take you onto the Lagmuck Sands. Just past this, an old iron gate leads left onto **Castlehill Point**.

6 Turn right down to another old gate back into the field. Follow its left edge to a signpost, for the path down left through scrub past Nelson's Grave (a drowned sailor, not the famous admiral). Head along the top edge of the rocky beach until a clear path runs through scrub just on the right to join the tarmac lane along the shore into **Rockcliffe**.

– To shorten

After checking tide tables, you can return from Portling along the mud and sand past the Needles Eye (4km with just 100m of climb, about 1hr 40min).

+ To lengthen

At the far end of Rockcliffe bay, turn right up a short lane and pick up the signposted Jubilee Path to Kippford, from where you can catch the bus back to Sandyhills. This extends the walk to 9.5km with 220m of climb, about 4hr.

Path up Knockendoch above Mid Glen

WALK 11
Criffel summit

Time 4½hr
Distance 9.5km (6 miles)
Climb 550m

A challenging circuit over Galloway's upstanding hill above one of its prettiest villages

Start/finish	*Mid Glen, at end of lane from New Abbey (at busy times, start at Sweetheart Abbey)*
Locate	*DG2 8DT ///searcher.cared.rents*
Cafes/pubs	*Beside Sweetheart Abbey (off route)*
Transport	*Buses from Dumfries to New Abbey*
Parking	*At Mid Glen, or at Sweetheart Abbey (adds 2.5km)*
Toilets	*In car park at Sweetheart Abbey, none on route*

Criffel stands alone, high above the Solway Firth. It used to be a notably boggy hill, but in 2020 a fine new path was built up it from Ardwall and the older path from New Abbey was improved. This route uses the New Abbey path, which gives a gentler ascent (though the section immediately below Knockendoch is steep and remains rough). From Criffel summit, the well-made new path is used for most of the descent. A linking path around the base of the hill by Loch Kindar completes the circuit.

New Abbey doorway

SHORT WALKS IN DUMFRIES & GALLOWAY

1 If you are starting from Sweetheart Abbey, head into the village and turn left, twice, above the Corn Mill. Take the path that short-cuts the lane zigzag, then follow the lane to Mid Glen. From the end of the lane at Mid Glen a track continues across a stream. Bear right

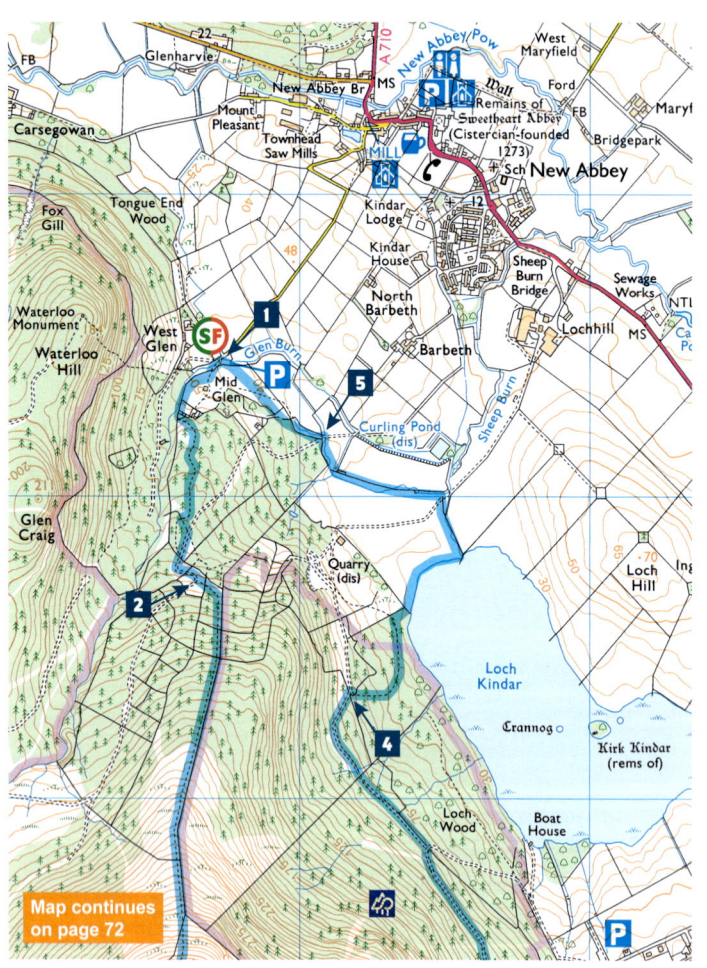

Slopes of Criffel above the Nith estuary

on a path to the right of **Mid Glen**, beside the stream at first. It runs to join a forest track, and in 200m this meets another track at a T-junction. Turn right up this for 200m, to the start of a well-made path ahead.

2 The path runs up through plantations then scattered trees, becoming steep and rough up to the preliminary summit **Knockendoch**. Here the path improves, along the left flank of the broad ridgeline. Just before the summit, join a wide gravel path to the top of **Criffel**, with its ancient cairn.

> Criffel is a huge lump of granite, melted in the heat of the collision of England with Scotland 400 million years ago. The granite gives the hill its upstanding, rounded shape. The name is Norse, meaning 'the crows' hill'. From the summit there are views across the sea to the English Lake District and the large Robin Rigg offshore windfarm.

3 Return along this wide gravel path, following it down the flank of the hill and into trees. Cross one forest track and at the second one turn left, signposted for New Abbey. After 600m, keep ahead on the main track. In another 500m, as the track bends left, a waymark arrow marks a green path down to the right.

4 The path, rather overgrown, leads down through scrubby bushes to a field beside **Loch Kindar**. Follow the loch shore left, round to a wall. Turn left alongside this, ignoring a track and gate on your right, to a gate at the field's far corner. Turn right through this, along a field edge to a track with a signpost. To return to New Abbey turn right along the track, then keep ahead through houses to the A710. A path to the left of the school leads round to the back of the abbey, with steps up left into its graveyard and the car park.

5 Turn left to a gate into woodland. At once fork right on a grassy track. Ignore a gate ahead and follow the track up left to a second gate. Through this, follow the long field ahead to a gate beside **Mid Glen**.

Sweetheart Abbey

Sweetheart Abbey with Criffel behind

The lovely ruins at New Abbey are worth a visit at the start or the end of the walk. The abbey was built around 1275 by Devorgilla, Countess Baliol. She was also responsible for the stone bridge across the Nith at Dumfries (Walk 13). It was nicknamed 'Sweetheart' because it was built in memory of her husband, John Baliol, and she is buried inside it, along with his heart. Most of the tower and the arched windows remain, as one of southern Scotland's most beautiful ruins. Even the long-term scaffolding and protective fence, in place at the time of writing, can't significantly spoil it.

Woods above Dalshinnie Glen

WALK 12
Mabie Forest

Start/finish	*Car park at Mabie Forest, south of Dumfries*
Locate	*DG2 8HA ///remembers.blunders.cobbled*
Cafes/pubs	*Mabie House Hotel 300m from start*
Transport	*Buses from Dumfries to the forest entrance*
Parking	*Forestry & Land Scotland car park (pay & display) at start*
Toilets	*At Sawmill 250m from start*

Time 3¼hr
Distance 8km (5 miles)
Climb 250m

A fairly strenuous woodland walk to a hidden pool and two views

Mabie Forest, just south of Dumfries, is mostly famous for mountain biking. But its 8 sq km also hold walking routes of different lengths, through mature fir trees and natural broadleaf woodland. The walks involve a fair bit of up and down, so that clearings give wide views out over the surrounding countryside, the Nith Estuary and the sea. The woods also hold a little swampy lochan.

Duckboard path at Dalshinnie Loch

SHORT WALKS IN DUMFRIES & GALLOWAY

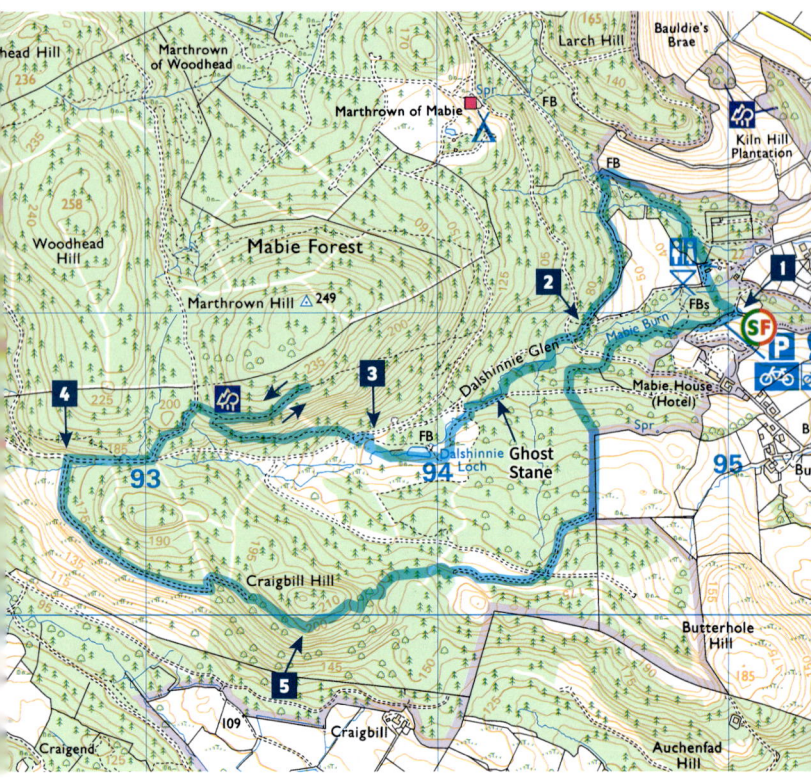

1 From the entrance end of the car park, a wide path leads down across a high footbridge over **Mabie Burn**, to reach an open shelter, the Sawmill. Turn left, signposted 'Dalshinnie Loch Trail', cross a small stream and turn uphill right of it. The first part of the walk currently has purple waymark posts. The path bends left, back across the stream, and joins a wider one contouring above open ground.

> ⓘ *Mabie is a haven for red squirrels and roe deer. Dalshinnie Loch is managed for that weirdly noisy night-flying bird the nightjar.*

WALK 12 – MABIE FOREST

Dalshinnie Glen

2 At the next junction turn uphill and cross a gravel track. In 50m turn left over Mabie Burn and head up left of it. Across the stream you will see the 'Ghost Stane' sculpture. Keep left of the burn to arrive at the corner of **Dalshinnie Loch**. Just before it, turn left on a duckboard path through swampy woodland. Keep left to pass a small pool and meet a wide, gravel path.

The 7Stanes mountain bike centres across southern Scotland each have their own 'Stane', or stone, sculpted by Gordon Young. Mabie's scupture, made of white marble, portrays a white nightie engraved with patterns from local lacemaking.

3 From here the rest of the route has red marker posts, mostly faded to bare brown. Turn left and cross a gravel track on a path slanting up to a viewpoint bench. If you turn right for 300m, you reach another bench high on **Marthrown Hill** with even better views to the Solway Firth. Return and follow the path ahead to a gravel forest road. Turn down left to a junction, then right for 400m, to a wide path turning down left.

Looking across to Criffel from Craigbill Hill

4 Follow the path, which runs past a picnic place with views over **Lochaber Loch**, then doubles back left to a path through natural woodland high on the side of **Craigbill Hill**. After a steep zig-zag climb, the path contours through the trees to a viewpoint looking out towards the sea and Criffel hill.

5 After a short, rough descent, the path runs east along a plateau for 600m. It bends left, then runs down north with open ground on the right. At junctions with forest tracks or bike trails just keep ahead, following the waymark posts. The path slants down through tall conifers above **Mabie Burn** to a junction. The car park is just up to the right.

> **– To shorten**
> At Waypoint 3 turn right, back past Dalshinnie Loch, and follow any path down Dalshinnie Glen, the valley of the Mabie Burn, back to the Sawmill (4km with 100m climb, about 1hr 30min).

WALK 13
Burns Walk, Dumfries

Start/finish	The Midsteeple, in the centre of Dumfries
Locate	DG1 2BH ///alleyway.declining.examples
Cafes/pubs	Pubs and cafes near start and more at Whitesands (Waypoint 3)
Transport	Train to Dumfries railway station 650m from start. Buses from Edinburgh, Glasgow, Carlisle to main bus stops at Waypoint 3
Parking	Large car park (free) at Brooms Road (a signpost marks steps down to join the route at the Burns House)
Toilets	Whitesands, alongside Devorgilla Bridge

Time 3¼hr
Distance 9.5km (6 miles)
Climb 30m

From the historic town of Dumfries along Robert Burns' favourite walk beside the River Nith

Scotland's poet Robert Burns spent his final years in Dumfries. Starting from the Midsteeple, an 18th-century town hall and prison with a distinctive tall steeple, this route follows his favourite walk alongside the wide River Nith, passing his home and favourite pub. When the river is in spate (look for brown water under Devorgilla Bridge), part of the walk upstream may be underwater, though this can be bypassed by climbing into a field.

Burns Walk, River Nith

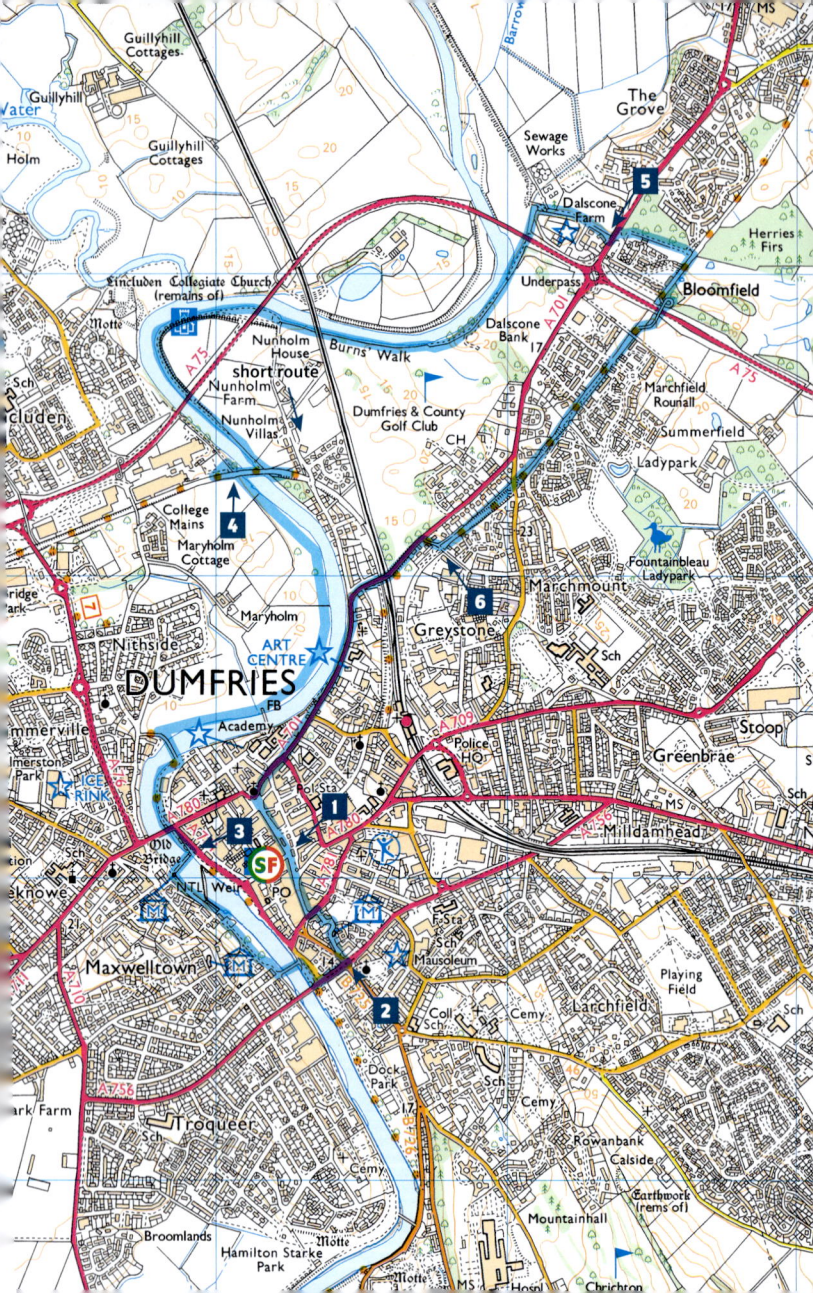

WALK 13 – BURNS WALK, DUMFRIES

Burns' Mausoleum, St Michael's churchyard

1 Head south down pedestrianised High Street. A narrow close on the left leads to Burns' favourite pub, the Globe Inn. Cross Nith Place and head up left into Burns Street opposite. This shadowy lane passes Burns House, where he lived from 1793 to his death three years later. It is now a small, free museum. Keep on along the street to a busy crossroads on the **A756**.

For Burns pilgrims, St Michael's Church, opposite, has Burns' Mausoleum in the back right corner of its kirkyard, surrounded by the decorated sandstone tombs of his neighbours.

2 Turn down right to the **River Nith** and cross the white-painted suspension bridge just upstream. Turn right past the Robert Burns Centre to the medieval Devorgilla Bridge (**Old Bridge**). The tiny Bridge House Museum at the nearer end of the bridge is worth 10 minutes of anybody's time. Cross the old bridge to the wide Whitesands, with pubs, cafes and bus stops.

The Burns Centre, a former watermill, houses a free exhibition on the poet's last years in Dumfries. A model of the town in the 1790s gives a preview of the walk ahead, and so does the 10-minute video, 'A Journey down the River Nith with Robert Burns'.

SHORT WALKS IN DUMFRIES & GALLOWAY

3 Turn upstream, with the river on your left. Pass under the Buccleuch Street Bridge, built during Burns' residence in the 1790s, and soon cross the blue-and-white footbridge just upstream. Steps on the right lead down to a grass path, which you follow upstream to the Queen of the South Viaduct, built for a former light railway.

4 Pass under the viaduct and go up the steps left to cross it. Continue upstream, now right of the river. For the next 2km you'll just follow the winding riverbank. After passing under the town bypass for the first time, you'll glimpse across the river the ruined Lincluden College Priory, founded by Archibald the Grim. After passing under the **A75** town bypass

> ⓘ *The ancient border of Galloway is the River Nith flowing through Dumfries. Anything east of the river is the 'Dumfries &' part of the region.*

Robert Burns

The Thames flows proudly to the sea,
Where royal cities stately stand;
But sweeter flows the Nith, to me …
That winding Stream I love so dear!

Robert Burns started life as a farm boy in Ayrshire. But by 1788 he'd earned enough from his poetry to buy himself a farm at Ellisland, just north of Dumfries. This wasn't a success, and in 1793 he got a job as exciseman, or customs officer, here in Dumfries – the town being at the time an important port. His poem 'The Deil's awa' wi' the Exciseman' suggests that he didn't enjoy the job; but ones such as 'The Banks of Nith' show that he came to love the town and its surroundings.

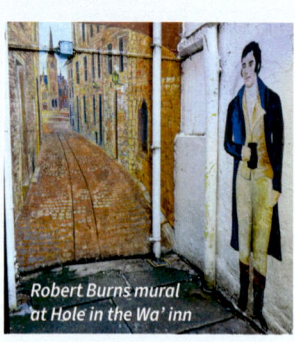
Robert Burns mural at Hole in the Wa' inn

WALK 13 – BURNS WALK, DUMFRIES

for the third time, keep ahead along a track away from the river. Turn right to pass through **Dalscone Farm**, a llama farm popular with children, to the **A701**.

5 Turn left and cross into a cul-de-sac, Bloomfield. At once bear left on a path, through woods then along the backs of houses, to meet a tarmac bike path. Turn right, then bear left to a spiral ramp onto a high bridge over the **A75**. Follow the leafy bike path back towards Dumfries for 1km and two road crossings, to reach a path crossroads.

6 Turn right, signposted for the railway station, up to join Edinburgh Road. Follow it ahead to the town centre. At the statue of Burns, turn left along High Street, past a close on the left leading to the second of Burns' pub hangouts, the Hole in the Wa', to arrive back at the Midsteeple.

Dumfries fountain and the Midsteeple

− To shorten
Between Waypoints 4 and 5, after passing under the A75 twice, at a small riverside car park take the lane that heads away from the river to join Edinburgh Road and follow it back to the start. But this does miss the best part of the Burns Walk (6km, about 2hr).

+ To lengthen
Before crossing the Queen of the South Viaduct at Waypoint 4, you could continue upstream for 800m, passing under the bypass, to visit the ruins of the 12th-century Lincluden Priory (1.5km there and back, about 30min).

Annan bridge and town hall

WALK 14
River Annan

Time 3¾hr
Distance 11km (6¾ miles)
Climb 60m

Some paths may be muddy on this long but soothing stroll beside Annan's big river

Start/finish	Annan Town Hall
Locate	DG12 6AQ ///outsmart.assist.pastels
Cafes/pubs	Cafes and pubs in Annan main street (pub at Brydekirk has closed)
Transport	Buses and trains to Annan from Carlisle or Dumfries, and buses from Brydekirk back to Annan
Parking	Car park (free) south of main street, small pull-in at west end of River Annan bridge
Toilets	50m east of Town Hall (turn right down Downies Street)

Grassy banks and beautiful woodlands line the wide, peaceful River Annan. Paths (sometimes muddy) and tracks on either bank give a natural walking route upstream to Brydekirk and back. Watch out for herons and, if you're really lucky, a kingfisher. Note that the two Victorian footbridges marked on maps above and below the A75 were swept away in the floods of autumn 2021, so there's no way before Brydekirk to cross the river to return on the other bank.

Beside the River Annan

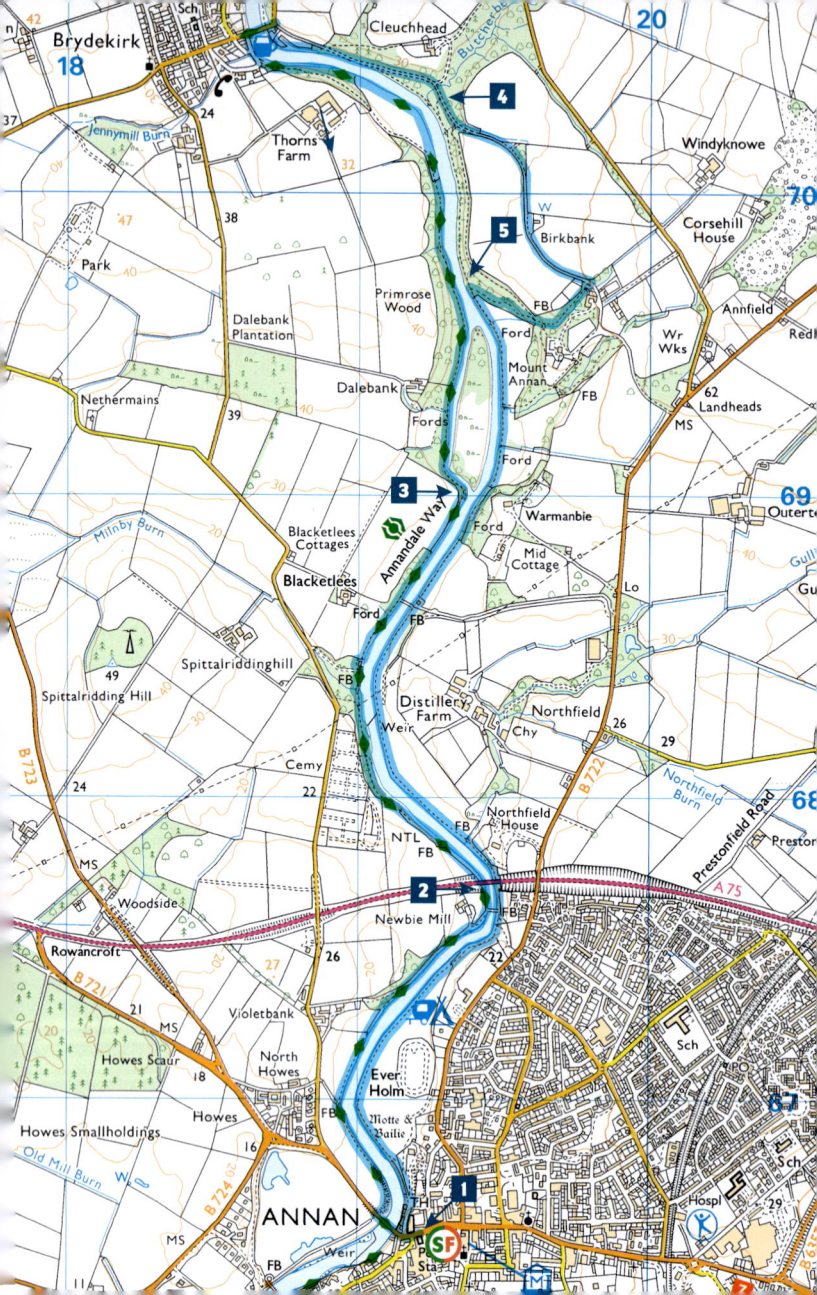

1 Behind the town hall is the road bridge at the western edge of **Annan**. Cross it and descend steps on the right to the **River Annan**. A footpath, rather muddy at first, runs upstream left of the river. After 1km you pass under the high viaduct of the **A75** Annan bypass.

2 Continue along the riverside, with markers for the Annandale Way. After 700m you pass the Caul – the Scots word for a **weir**. At 1.5km from the bypass bridge, the path bends left alongside the bottom end of a large river island. The bench here is a good turning point for a shorter out-and-back walk.

3 The path continues up the riverbank, through the attractive **Primrose Wood**, to **Brydekirk**. Cross the road bridge here and take a small path on the right at the bridge end. The path soon joins a leafy track. After a riverside shelter hut, the track eases away from the river to cross a stone bridge over **Butcherbeck Burn**. In another 100m, a wide path forks down right off the track.

4 Here you have two choices. Simplest is to take the path on the right, rejoining the riverbank to continue downstream. Alternatively, as shown on the map, you can stay on the track, which rises through fields, with wider views. After **Birkbank** cottage,

Path below Mount Annan

and just before a farm, a gate on the right has a 'walkers welcome' sign. Go through this to join a small, rough path leading down through woods. The path runs to the right of a creek, then above the foot of the wood, to a second shelter hut at the riverside.

Annan at dusk

5 Continue downstream on good paths, passing the Caul and going under the **A75** viaduct. At the far end of a riverside park, a short lane leads up to the town hall.

> **— To shorten**
>
> Turn back from the river island (5km there and back – about 1hr 30min).

Annandale Distillery

Half a mile north of the town is Annan's Victorian distillery. It closed in 1918, but re-opened in the same building in 2014, one of only two single-malt whisky distilleries in southern Scotland. Some of Annandale's whisky is peaty-flavoured in the usual whisky way: this is 'Man o' Sword', named after Annandale-born Robert the Bruce. Some of it, however, is peat-free: this is 'Man o' Words', commemorating Robert Burns. Distillery tours (which must be pre-booked) end with a tasting where you can determine what a difference moving that single letter S makes.

The distillery's former malting floor, under the distinctive ventilator chimney, has been converted into a cafe. Disappointingly there's no footpath to it from the town or riverbank.

WALK 15
Langholm and Potholm Hill

Start/finish	*Riverside on A7 at north edge of Langholm*
Locate	*DG13 0EP ///parkway.journey.providing*
Cafes/pubs	*Hotels in Langholm, cafe 500m north on A7*
Transport	*Buses to Langholm centre from Edinburgh and Carlisle*
Parking	*Car park at start*
Toilets	*In car park*

Time 3¾hr
Distance 9.5km (6 miles)
Climb 250m

A moderate hill climb rewarded by outstanding views along two glens and over the town

The Esk is the easternmost of the region's big rivers. Langholm, in this eastern glen, lies well away from the green coastal country and inside the Southern Uplands, hemmed in by tall, grassy hills. At 310m Potholm Hill is one of the smaller ones, but slotted as it is in between two rivers it has great views up both valleys, as well as down onto the town. For contrast, the walk starts alongside the River Esk, guided by the big river but, initially at least, away from the waymarked routes.

Stile on Castle Hill

Langholm High Street and town hall

WALK 15 – LANGHOLM AND POTHOLM HILL

1 At the north edge of the car park, cross **Ewes Bridge**. In 100m take a gate on the left into parkland and double back left beside the wall. The tarmac path runs downstream beside Ewes Water, then upstream beside River Esk to reach the Jubilee footbridge. Alternatively you can shortcut across the grass to the tree clump containing ruined Langholm Castle.

2 Cross the bridge and turn upstream on an earth path under trees. After 500m re-cross the river on the grey-arched **Duchess Bridge** and turn left to join the wide riverside path. After 800m the path bends right and becomes a track. Ignore side-tracks to the left then right, to reach the outbuildings of **Holmhead**. From here on there are waymarks for Langholm walk no. 4.

SHORT WALKS IN DUMFRIES & GALLOWAY

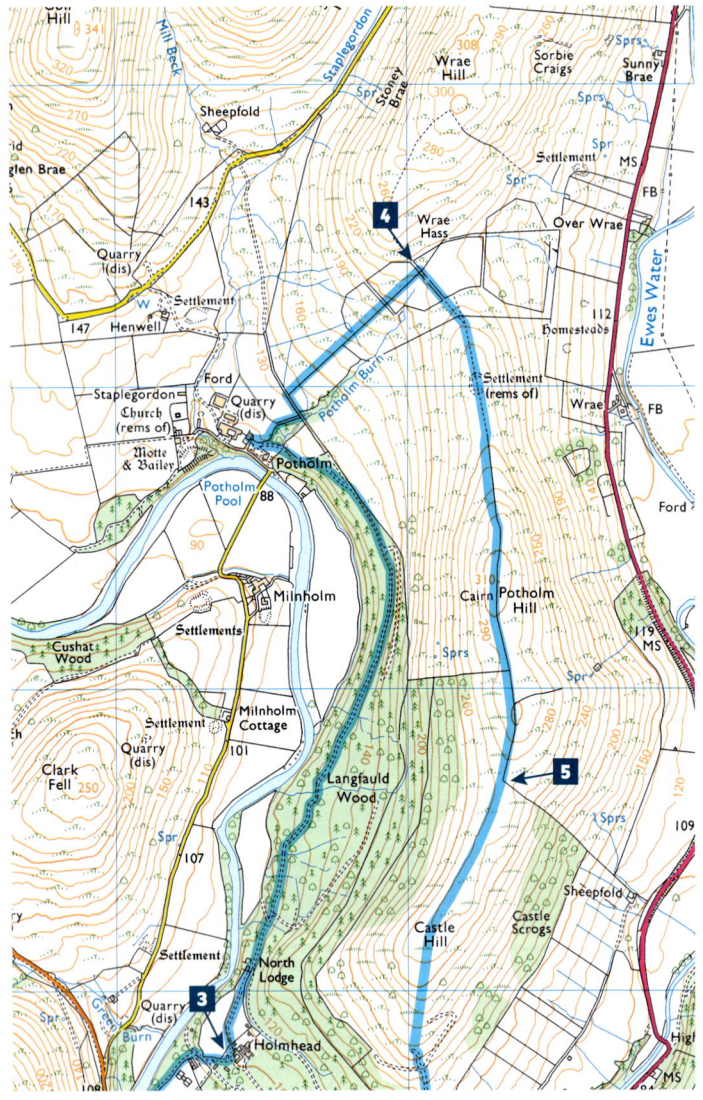

WALK 15 – LANGHOLM AND POTHOLM HILL

Potholm Hill seen from Wrae Hass

3 Turn left on the earth track, soon with views over the River Esk. After 2km, watch out for a fork down left, which leads to buildings at **Potholm**. Take the track to the right, which climbs then bends left to a gate with stile. Having crossed this turn up right, on a quad bike track beside the fence, to the wide saddle of **Wrae Hass**.

The ancient Scots word 'hass' means a col or saddle, especially one used as a pass. In northern England the spelling 'hause' is common.

4 Turn right through a gate onto open hillside. There will be no more waymarks on the high ground ahead. A faint path follows the low remains of a wall, up through a gate with a stile, then along a level section and up **Potholm Hill**. Keep ahead along the hill crest to a wall corner with a gate and ladder stile. Continue right of the wall, which descends to a corner.

The little grass hollows at Potholm summit and alongside this wall are former quarries yielding stones of the wall itself. They make sheltered picnic spots.

5 From the corner a very faint path leads on along the hill crest, southwest, over the slight rise of

Cheviot lambs above Langholm

Castle Hill. As the slope steepens, descend straight towards **Langholm** town on a track formed by tractor wheels between scattered thorn trees. Above a crossing wall, the track bends left to a gate and ladder stile. At a T-junction turn down left. The track turns down to the right and becomes tarmac as it descends steeply to **Ewes Bridge** and back to the car park.

− To shorten

For a short, pushchair-friendly walk turn right at Holmhead, joining its tarmac driveway back to Ewes Bridge (3.7km, about 40min). For a longer alternative without the climb, at Potholm turn left, waymarked as 'Langholm walk no. 2'. Across the River Esk follow the tarmac lane for 2km, then a rough path left leads above the river to Duchess Bridge (9.5km with only 60m climb, saves 30min).

+ To lengthen

Above Potholm continue along the track then a road to a cattle grid, then turn up steep grass to cross Wrae Hill. Turn down grass slopes to Wrae Hass and rejoin the main route (12km with 350m climb, about 5hr).

USEFUL INFORMATION

Tourism bodies

Scotland Tourism www.visitscotland.com
Galloway Forest Park www.forestryandland.gov.scot and search 'Galloway Forest Park'
Historic Environment Scotland www.historicenvironment.scot
National Trust for Scotland www.nts.org.uk

Tourist information centres

The main tourist information centre is at Whitesands, Dumfries and is open year-round. Smaller local information centres are at Stranraer, Kirkcudbright, Castle Douglas and Gretna Gateway.

Travel

Rail www.scotrail.com
Bus and rail www.travelinescotland.com

Accommodation

www.booking.com
www.trivago.co.uk
www.airbnb.co.uk

Further reading

Walking the Galloway Hills (Cicerone, 2019) has a selection of more challenging walks in the Galloway Highlands.

Dumfries & Galloway Council has published a useful leaflet of half a dozen local walks: these cover Annan, Castle Douglas, Dalbeattie, Dumfries, Gatehouse, the Glenkens, Kirkcudbright, Machars (Wigtown), Moffat, Newton Stewart, Stranraer and Thornhill. Download them at D&Gonline www.dumfries-and-galloway.co.uk (search 'Walks and Walking Dumfries and Galloway').

© Ronald Turnbull 2023
First edition 2023
ISBN: 978 1 78631 172 6

Printed in China on responsibly sourced paper on behalf of Latitude Press Ltd.
A catalogue record for this book is available from the British Library.

© Crown copyright and database rights 2023 OS AC0000810376
All photographs are by the author unless otherwise stated.

CICERONE

Cicerone Press, Juniper House, Murley Moss, Oxenholme Road,
Kendal, Cumbria, LA9 7RL

www.cicerone.co.uk

Updates to this Guide

While every effort is made to ensure the accuracy of guidebooks as they go to print, changes can occur during the lifetime of an edition. Any updates that we know of for this guide will be on the Cicerone website (www.cicerone.co.uk/1172/updates), so please check before planning your trip. We also advise that you check information about transport, accommodation and shops locally. We are always grateful for updates, sent by email to updates@cicerone.co.uk or by post to Cicerone, Juniper House, Murley Moss, Oxenholme Road, Kendal, LA9 7RL.

Register your book: To sign up to receive free updates, special offers and GPX files where available, register your book at www.cicerone.co.uk.